This notebook belongs to a
WEREWOLF
whose human name is

_____

This notebook has pages designed for different purposes. However, you can use it any way you want. After all, YOU'RE A WEREWOLF!!!

The only rule regarding this notebook:
DO NOT let it fall into the wrong hands.

Copyright ©Sir Brody Books, 2019
ISBN 978-1-951551-01-8
Cover art from D.K. Brantley's Plain Old Frankie

Remember, being a werewolf

doesn't make you less human.

Being a werewolf

makes you more awesome.

Write about your scariest transformation. Who was there? How did it feel?

Draw your favorite place to be when you wolf out.

I'd rather

be howling.

If you told one friend your secret, who would it be? How would you break the news?

If someone turned you into a werewolf, draw him or her.

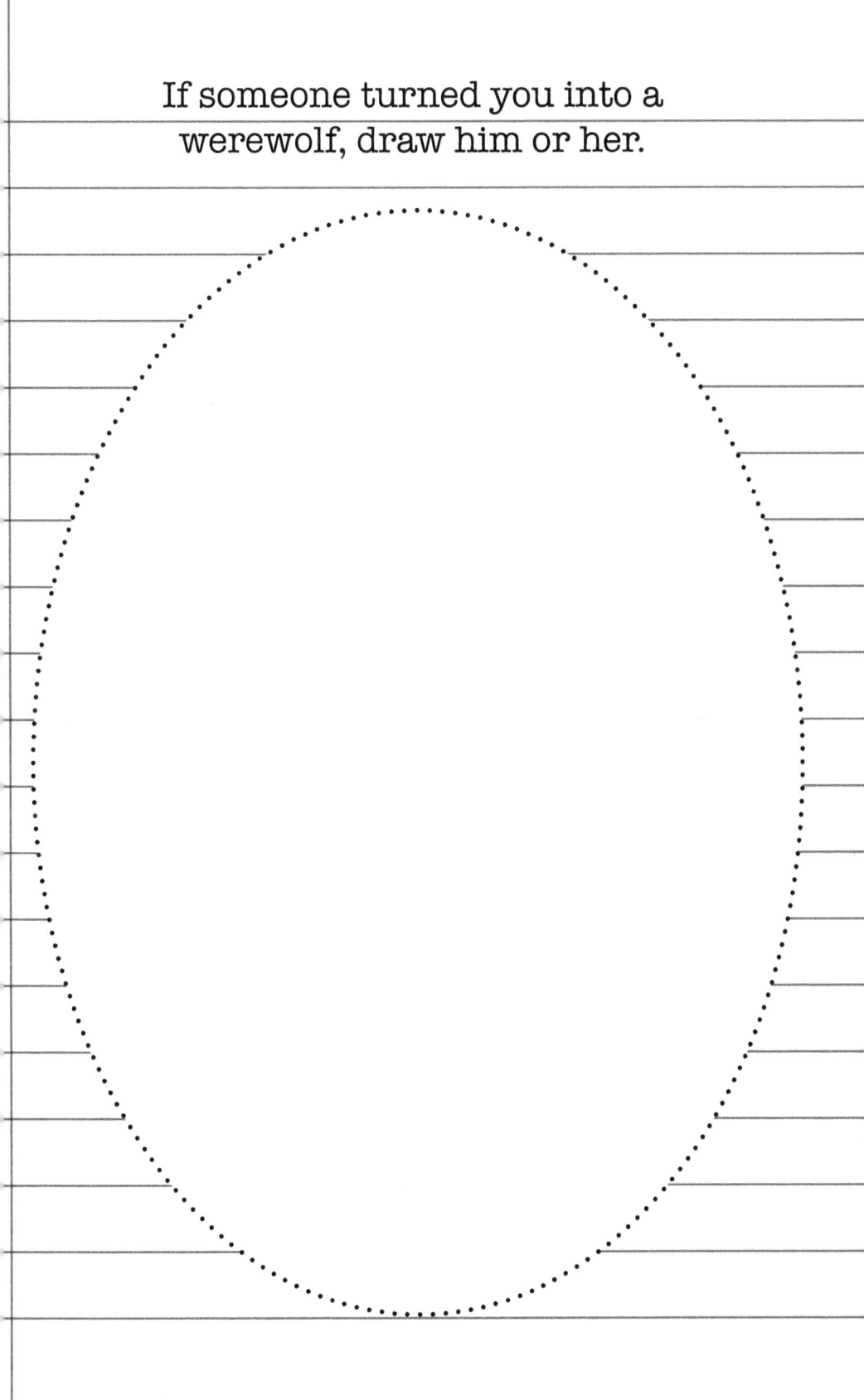

There's no moon

like a full moon.

What are the 5 best things about being a werewolf?

1.

2.

3.

4.

5.

Werewolf paws come in all shapes and sizes. What does yours look like?

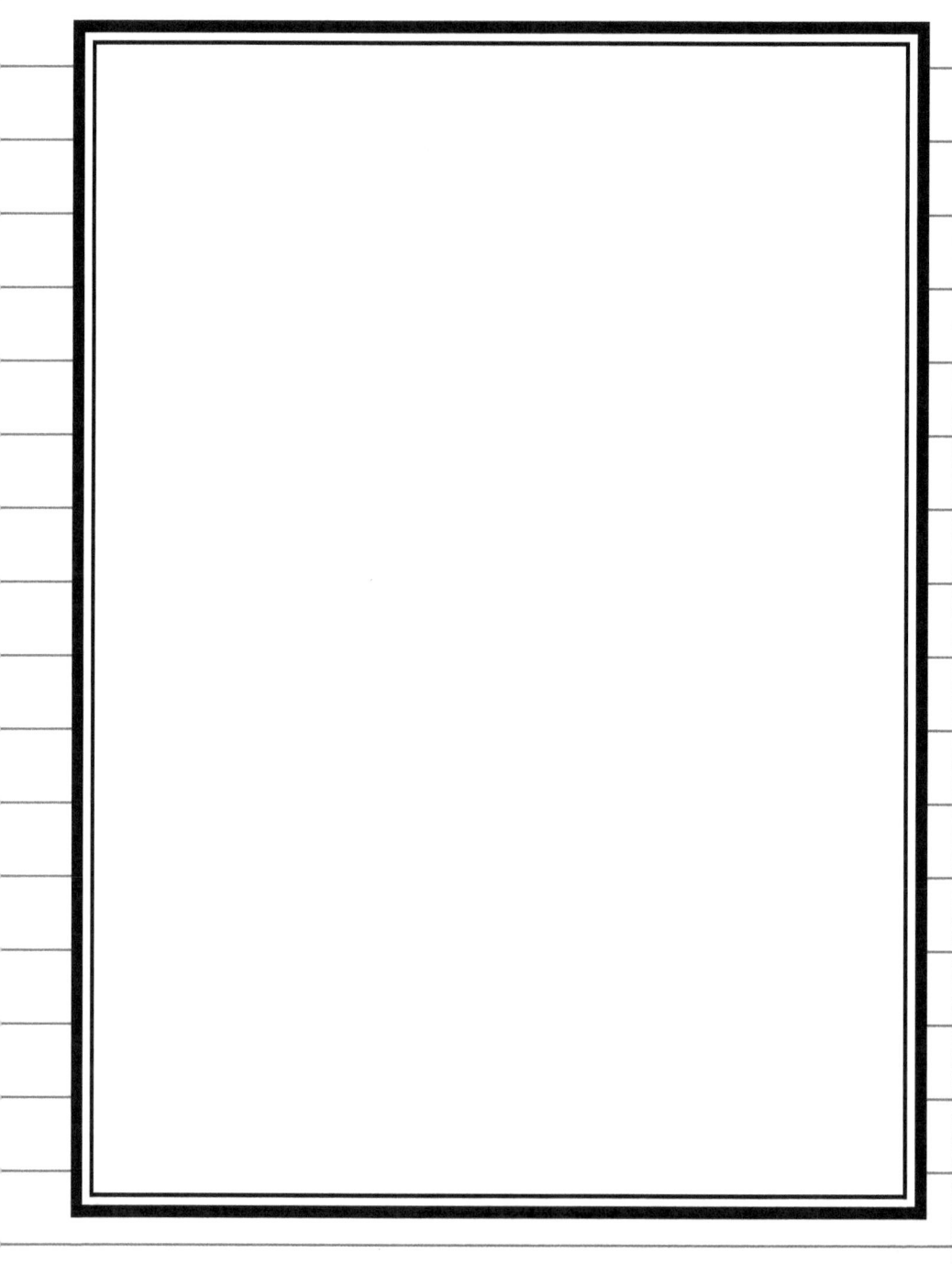

Draw a close-up of your favorite claw.

The best family

comes in a pack.

What are the 5 worst things about being a werewolf?

1.

2.

3.

4.

5.

What is your favorite toy when in wolf form? Draw it.

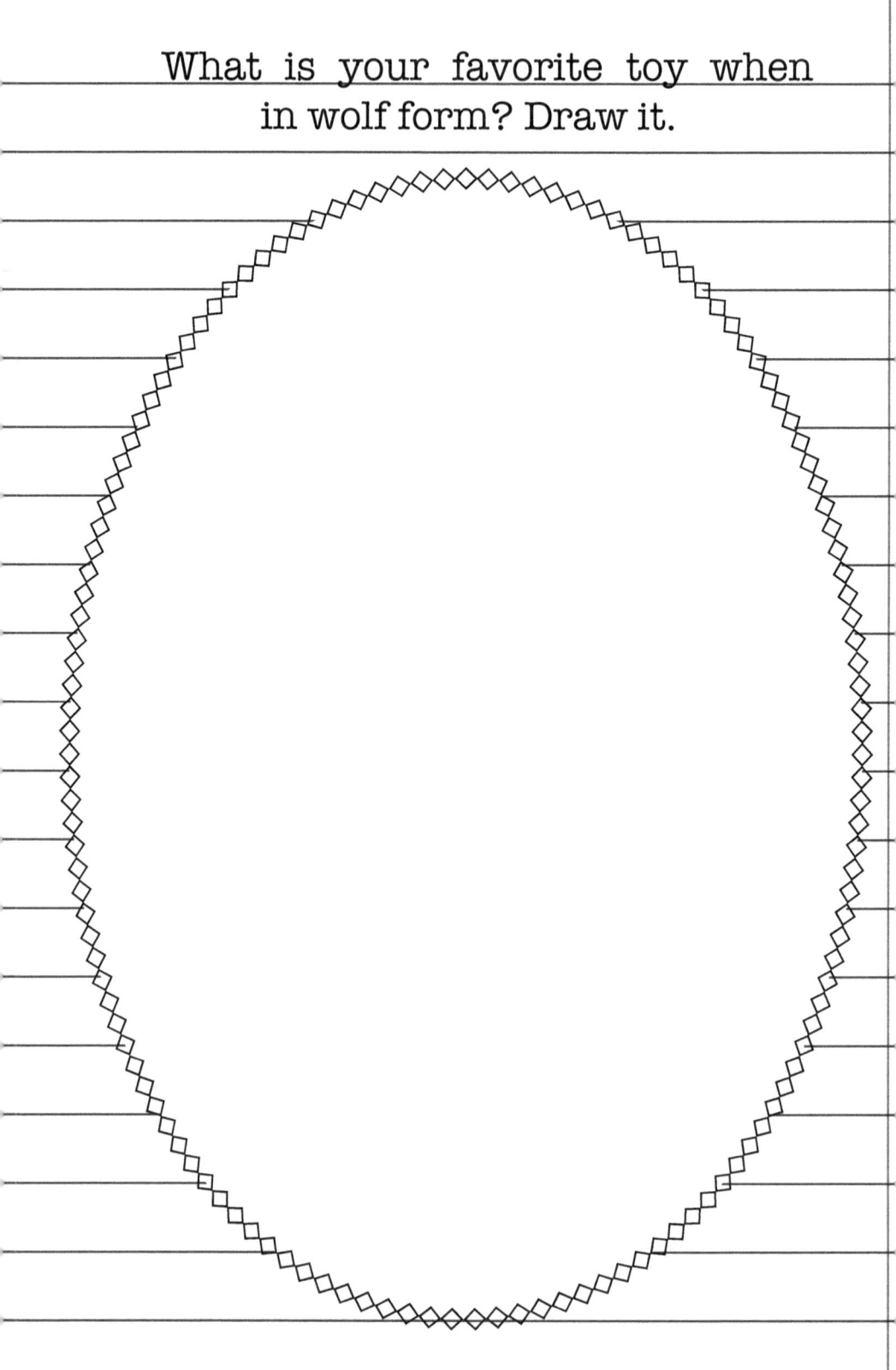

Werewolves don't need to be feared

unless they're angry.

How does it make you feel to be called a monster? Powerful? Sad? EXPLAIN!!!

What's the first sign you're transforming?
Do your ears tingle? Heart race? Draw it.

To err is human,

to wolf divine.

What do you wish people knew about werewolves?

Draw what you look like in human form.

A werewolf's hearing is

16 times better than normal humans.

Do you prefer to be called a werewolf or lycanthrope? Why?

Do you prefer full moons on a clear or cloudy night? Draw it!

The best baths

take place in cool streams.

Describe your craziest night as a werewolf.
Where did you go? What did you do?

Draw your favorite food when in human form.

Draw your favorite food when in wolf form.

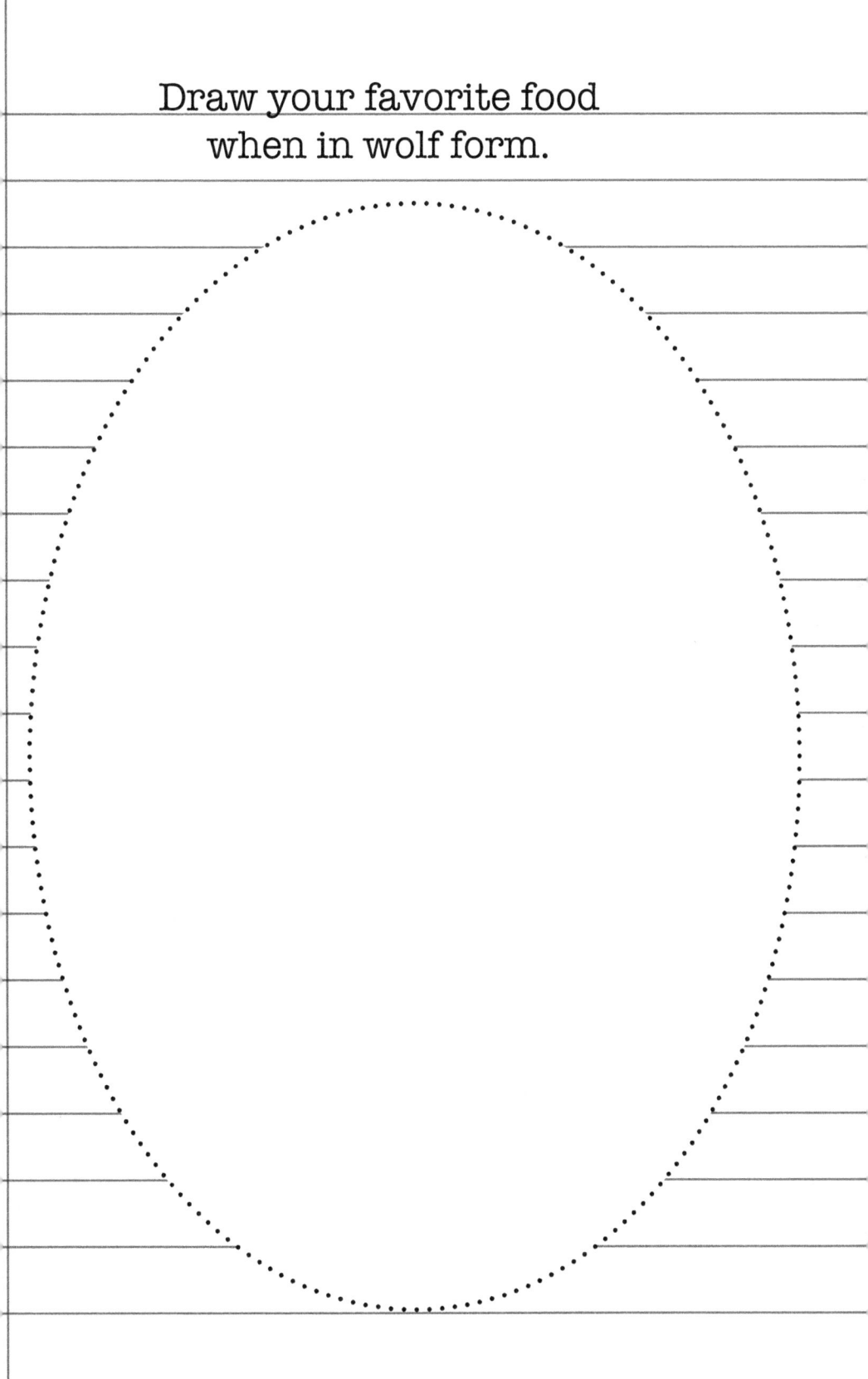

There can only be

one alpha.

What is the pecking order of your pack?

Alpha Male:

Alpha Female:

Beta Male:

Beta Female:

Delta:

Lead Warrior:

Warriors:

Hunters:

Healers:

Omega Male:

Omega Female:

What does your pack den look like? Draw it below.

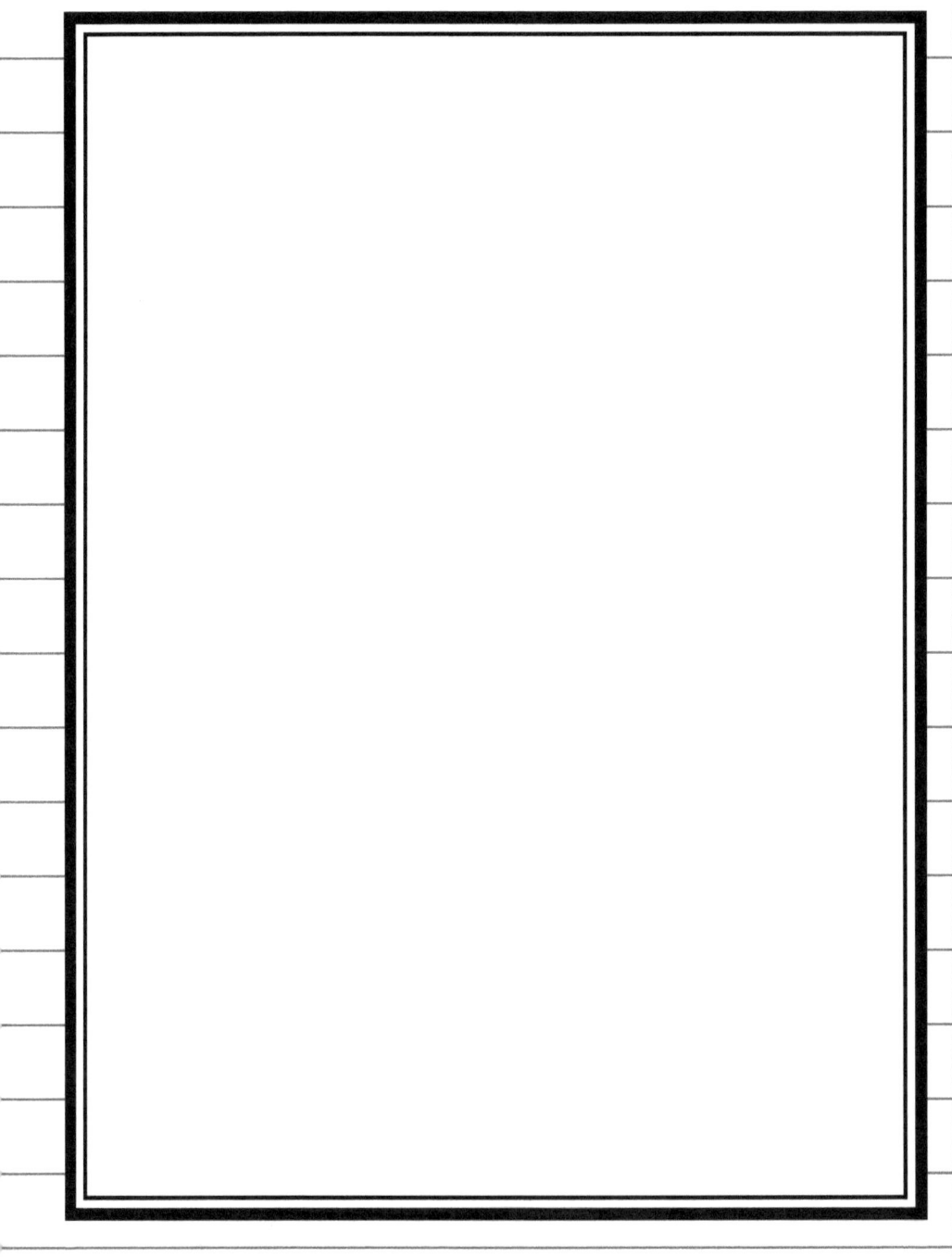

What does your human bedroom look like? Draw it below.

I don't want to live

in a world without werewolves.

Write a story in which your favorite celebrity admits to being a werewolf.

Being a werewolf can be dangerous. Draw your biggest werewolf-related fear.

One difference between humans and werewolves:

Werewolves don't hunt for sport.

If you were born a werewolf, when did you learn about your wolf identity?

Do you know any other werewolves?
Draw him or her!

Do you wish someone was a werewolf? Draw him or her!

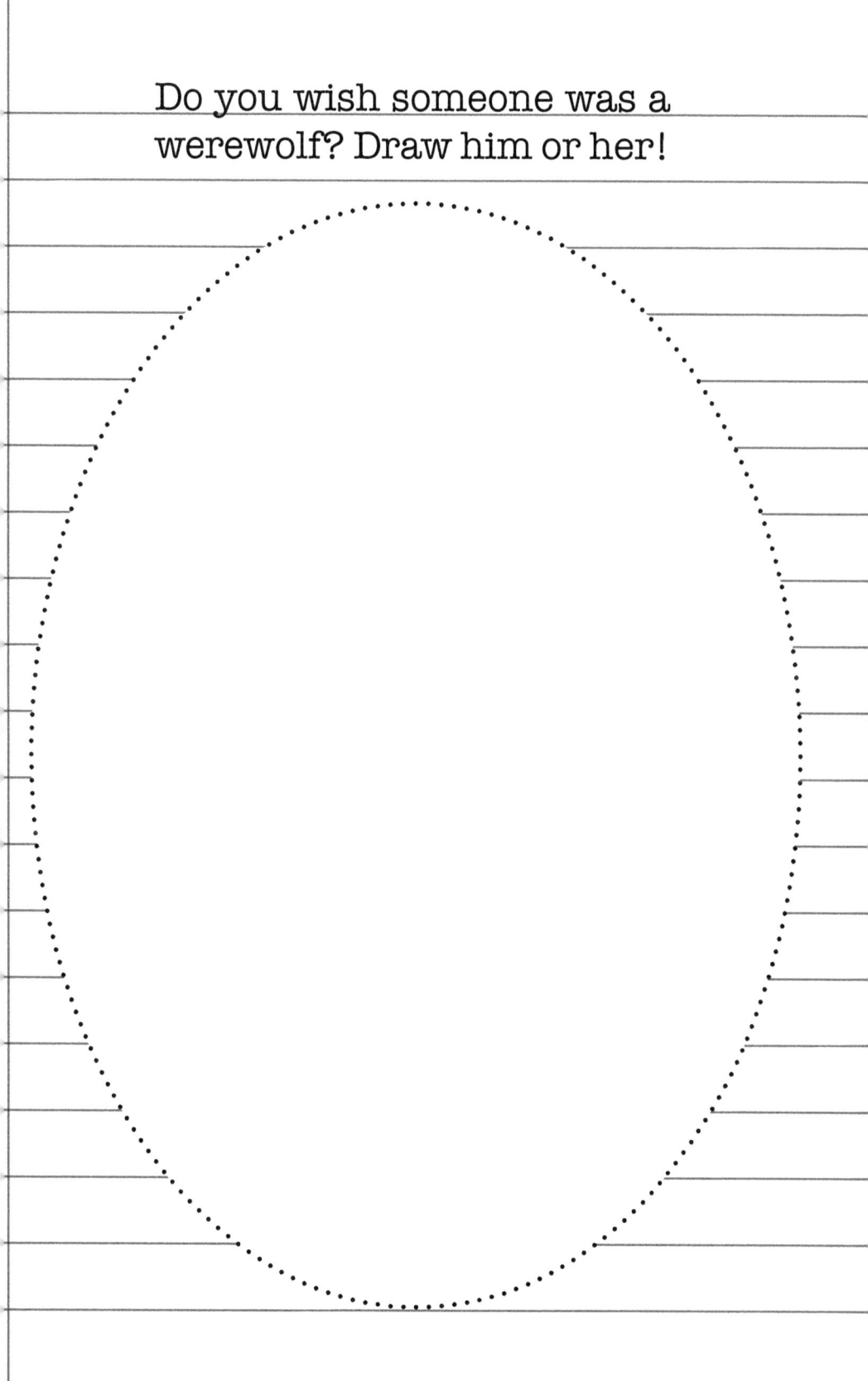

A lone wolf

is a lonely wolf.

How does being a werewolf help you be a better person?

Draw yourself as a young werewolf pup.

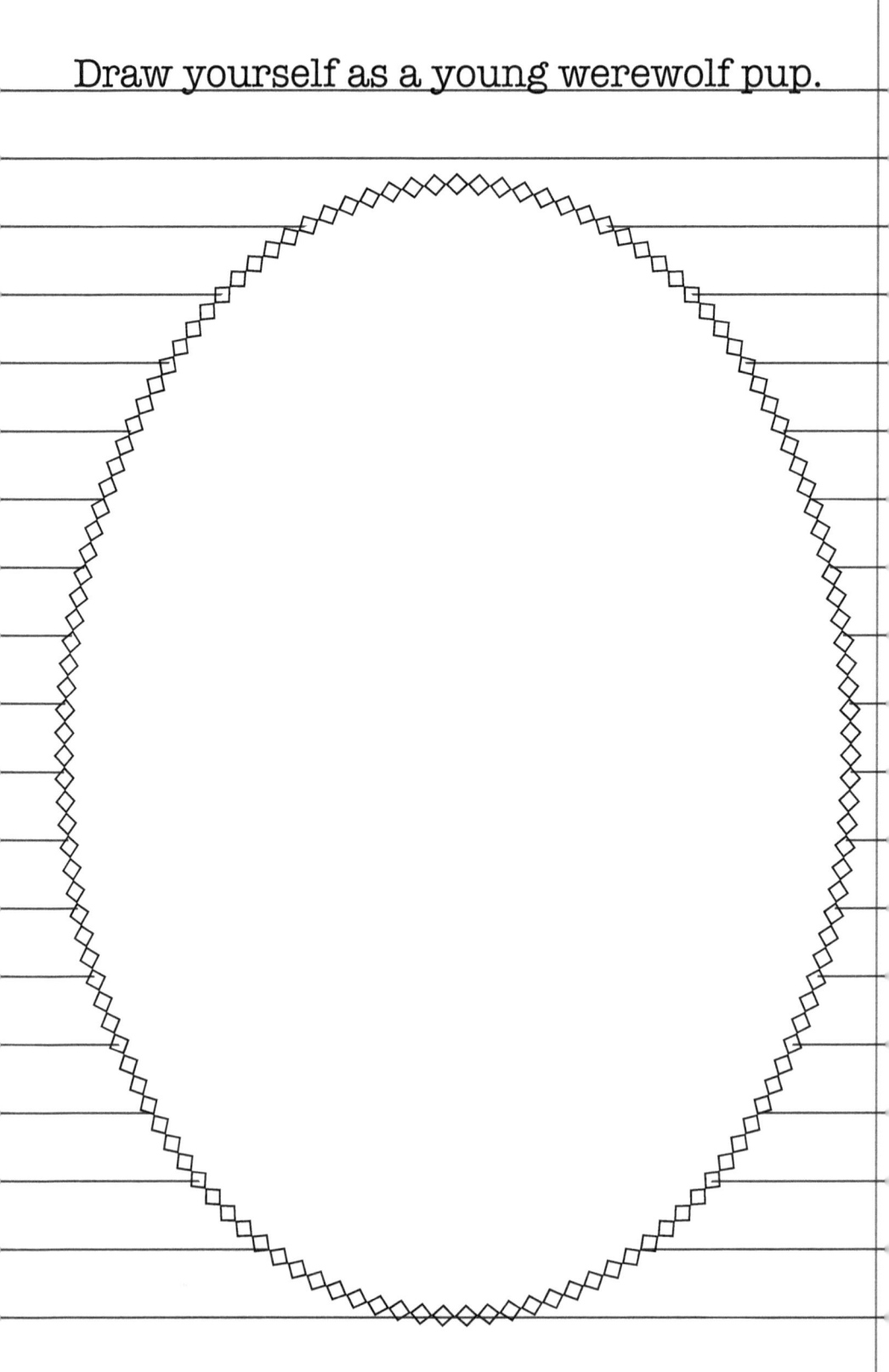

Draw yourself as an old, wise werewolf.

www.ingramcontent.com/pod-product-compliance
Lightning Source LLC
Chambersburg PA
CBHW052100110526
44591CB00013B/2294